God's Precious Jewels

God's Precious Jewels

A Study of the
Stones on the
Breastplate of
Judgment

C.K. FLETCHER

REDEMPTION PRESS

© 2010 by C. K. Fletcher. All rights reserved.

Published by Redemption Press, PO Box 427, Enumclaw, WA 98022.

Printed in the United States of America

No part of this publication may be reproduced, stored in a retrieval system, or transmitted in any way by any means—electronic, mechanical, photocopy, recording, or otherwise—without the prior permission of the copyright holder, except as provided by USA copyright law.

Scripture references are taken from the King James Version of the Bible.

ISBN 13: 978-1-63232-739-0

Library of Congress Catalog Card Number: 2004100875

TABLE OF CONTENTS

Acknowledgements 7
Introduction 9

Chapter 1 13
Chapter 2 17
Chapter 3 21
Chapter 4 27
Chapter 5 35

ACKNOWLEDGEMENTS

To my heavenly Father who continuously reminds me that, "... the testimony of the Lord is sure, making wise the simple." (Psalm 19:7)

To my earthly father, who lives a life of faith before me.

To my siblings, who always encourage me and are so, so supportive.

To my husband, who is my friend, my confidant, and my best critic.

And also to my pastors and Sunday School teacher, whose teachings and spiritual guidance have been very instrumental in the development of this book.

INTRODUCTION

One of our Sunday school lessons involved studying the tabernacle of the Old Testament and its properties. A part of that lesson included the high priest and his garments. Our Sunday school teacher asked us to pick an item, do research, and present our findings to the class. I chose the breastplate of judgment. In Exodus 28, God gave Moses explicit instructions regarding how the breastplate should be made, who should wear it, and why it should be worn. God told Moses in Exodus 28:29:

> *And Aaron shall bear the names of the children of Israel in the breastplate of judgment upon his heart, when he goeth in unto the holy place, for a memorial before the Lord continually . . . and you shall put settings of stones in it, four rows of stones . . . and the stones shall have the names of the sons of Israel . . . each one with its own name; they shall be according to the twelve tribes.*

Three things about this verse intrigued me. First of all, the phrase, *breastplate of judgment*. Secondly, the word *memorial*: what was there about the names of the children of Israel and the breastplate of judgment that God wanted to remember? Thirdly, why did God want the high priest to wear the breastplate of judgment in the Holy Place?

I was also curious about the Holy Place, where Aaron was to wear this breastplate of judgment; what does that have to do with me today? I found that the Old Testament reveals that Aaron, the high priest, was to enter into the Holy of Holies annually to atone for the sins of the people. But in the New Testament, Christ Jesus ushered in a new and better covenant.

Hebrews 9 reveals to us that . . . *neither by the blood of goats and calves, but by his own blood he entered in once into the holy place having obtained eternal redemption for us.* . . . That chapter went on to say that . . . *"Christ is not entered into the holy places made with hands, which are the figures of the true; but into heaven itself, now to appear in the presence of God for us.* . . . By now I was excited! Christ, our High Priest, is in the presence of God (the holiest of holy), and He is continually bearing our names upon His heart before God.

My research then led me to Malachi 3:16–17 which says: *"Then they that feared the Lord spake often one to another: and the Lord hearkened; and heard it, and a book of remembrance was written before Him for them that feared the Lord, and that thought upon His name. 'And they shall be mine,' said the Lord of Hosts, 'in that day when I make up my jewels."*

While reading this my heart cried out, "When You say seek My face, Thy face will I seek. Father, what did it mean when the Word said, ". . . *they that feared the Lord"?* And my Father in His gracious mercy answered me. Webster's dictionary says fear means to *reverence.* And reverence means to have a profound and adoring respect for someone, to the point where you deliberately posture your heart to seek one's favor and bow to one's wishes.

When I read this, my heart almost burst from the revelation I

Introduction

received. It gave me a glimpse of the heart of God. In this verse our God was sending us a love note! His heart was touched by the fact that there were those of His people who feared (reverenced) Him, gathered together, thought about Him, and spoke about Him. The Lord heard this, and His heart was made glad. He wanted to memorialize the fact that there were those who demonstrated love for Him, freely and without prompting. His heart spontaneously said, *"they shall be mine . . . in that day when I make up my jewels."*

I believe *that day* God spoke of are the perilous times we live in now.

I began to write the narrative of this study on September 11, 2001. I worked the night shift at that time and had been off the night before. I rose early on the morning of September 11th and spent some time with the Lord and then sat at the computer and began to write. I wrote all morning until about 12:00 noon when my husband called and asked if I had heard the news. I didn't know what was going on, because I didn't have the television on. I was communing with God.

God's heart rang out to me in Isaiah 62:1–3: *"For Zion's sake I will not hold my peace, and for Jerusalem's sake I will not rest, until the righteousness thereof go forth as brightness, and the salvation thereof as a lamp that burneth. And the Gentiles shall see thy righteousness, and all kings thy glory: and thou shalt be called by a new name, which the mouth of the Lord shall name.*

"Thou shalt also be a crown of glory in the hand of the Lord, and a royal diadem in the hand of thy God."

I had asked the Lord, "Father, what is a *diadem*?" Webster's dictionary states that a diadem is a crown of royalty exemplifying power and dignity.

Our Father is saying in these verses that He was not going to *rest* until the righteousness and the salvation of His people—His royal priesthood that exemplified His might, power and dignity—would burn like the brightness of a lamp for the world to see! Can you hear the passion in our Master's heart? Oh, imagine the joy that He felt when He noted that there were those who agreed with His heart, agreed that righteousness and salvation shall reign!

God also is saying in Exodus 19:5 "*. . . now therefore, if ye will obey my voice indeed, and keep my covenant, then ye shall be a peculiar treasure unto me above all people . . .*" The Scriptures also reveal in Zechariah 9:16: "*. . . and the Lord their God shall save them in that day as the flock of his people: for they shall be as the stones of a crown, lifted up as an ensign upon his land.*" Did you know that the archaic definition of *ensign* is a banner carried at the top of a pole and used to mark a rallying point in a battle? It has never been more evident that mankind is in a spiritual battle than on September 11, 2001. God is looking for a people who will be an ensign of His love, might, and power in the midst of the battle between good and evil. This is not a fairy tale like *The Lord of the Rings*. This is a true battle between Satan and God for control over God's creation. Oh, to be like the stones of a crown in His eyes; to be lifted up as an ensign over His land!

This study of the stones in the breastplate of judgment will reveal to us what is required to be a precious jewel in God's eyes, what is required to be His royal priesthood, and a mighty soldier in His army.

CHAPTER 1

In Exodus 28 God gave explicit instructions regarding how to make the holy garments the high priest was to wear. The breastplate of judgment is part of those priestly garments. This chapter also reveals that the breastplate of judgment was to be made of four rows of stones, with three stones in each row. God gave explicit orders what stones were to be used; and the order in which they were to be placed. He stated, "... *thou shalt set in it settings of stones, even four rows of stones: the first row shall be a sardius, a topaz, and a carbuncle ... the second row shall be an emerald, a sapphire, and a diamond ... the third row a liqure, an agate, and an amethyst ... and the fourth row a beryl, and an onyx, and a jasper.*"

God is a God of order. Everything He does He does for a reason; and in each thing He does there's a message for us all. Therefore, there's a message hidden in this breastplate of judgment and in the manner in which its stones are set.

In my endeavor to find this hidden message, my research led to the development of Table I.

TABLE I

STONES	STONE'S PROPERTIES	SON OF ISRAEL	MEANING OF NAME	BLESSING OF JACOB ON HIS SONS (GENESIS 49)
		First Row		
Sardius	Corundum; red, hard tough stone, can be used as an abrasive (used for smoothing and polishing)	Reuben	Behold a Son	My first born, my might, the beginning of strength, the excellency of dignity and power
Topaz	Salt of aluminum which has good electrical and thermal conductivity, high reflectivity and resistive to oxidation	Simeon	Hearing	
Carbuncle	A garnet, red, precious stone that also is an abrasive (used for smoothing and polishing)	Levi	To be joined to; to abide with	
		Second Row		
Emerald	A beryl, which is a salt of beryllium and aluminum used as a hardening agent in alloy (a metal mixed with a more valuable metal to give it durability)	Judah	Praise	Thy hand shall be in the neck of thine enemies
Sapphire	A corundum; massive crystal used as an abrasive (smoothing and polishing agent)	Dan	To Judge	Shall judge his people
Diamond	One of the hardest stones in the world; used as an abrasive for smoothing and polishing	Naphtali	My Wrestling	Is a hind let loose; he giveth goodly words
		Third Row		
Ligure	Also called zircon; precious orange stone used in alloys, has the capacity to be resistant to corrosion	Gad	A Troop	He shall overcome at the last
Agate	Fine grained transparent crystal (A Quartz) used in industry to set right a frequency or keep it on course	Asher	Blessed	His bread shall be fat, and he shall yield royal dainties
Amethyst	Purple crystalized quartz, used as an abrasive as well as an agent used to set a frequency or keep it on course	Issachar	Hired for Payment	A Strong ass crouching down between two burdens. . . . And bowed his shoulder to bear and became a servant unto tribute
		Fourth Row		
Beryl	A salt of beryllium and aluminum used as a hardening agent in alloy (a metal mixed with a more valuable metal to give it durability)	Zebulun	To Dwell With	Shall dwell at the haven of the sea; and he shall be for a haven of ships; and his border shall be unto zidon
Onyx	Translucent quartz in parallel layers of different colors; used to set right a frequency or keep it on course	Joseph	The Lord Shall Add	Fruitful bough whose branches run over the wall
Jasper	Translucent quartz of many colors, especially green: used to set right a frequency or keep it on course	Benjamin	Son of the Right Hand	Shall ravin as a wolf in the morning shall devour the prey and at night he shall divide the spoil

Chapter One

Some scholars of the Bible say that the names on the stones in the breastplate of judgment are inscribed according to the tribes that were listed in Numbers when Israel's first census was taken. However, that listing of the tribes leaves out Levi and Joseph. This study is based on what was done in Exodus 39:14, when the priest's clothing were actually made. That Scripture says: *"And the stones were according to the names of the children of Israel, twelve, according to their names, like the engravings of a signet, every one with his name, according to the twelve tribes."*

Therefore, this study of the stones in the breastplate of judgment includes the names of all of the sons of Israel in the order they were born to him.

When I looked at this table as a whole, several things jumped out at me. The first thing that occurred to me was that each stone with its corresponding property, the meaning of the name of the sons of Israel, and the blessing the sons received from their father, contained a message in itself. If you look at the meaning of the names of the first three sons of Israel in the first row of stones; you will see the hidden message: *Behold a son, hearing, be joined to, abide with.*

Isn't God awesome!

CHAPTER 2

TABLE II

STONES	STONE'S PROPERTIES	SON OF ISRAEL	MEANING OF NAME	BLESSING OF JACOB ON HIS SONS (GENESIS 49)
		First Row		
Sardius	Corundum; red, hard tough stone, can be used as an abrasive (used for smoothing and polishing)	Reuben	Behold a Son	My first born, my might, the beginning of strength, the excellency of dignity and power
Topaz	Salt of aluminum which has good electrical and thermal conductivity, high reflectivity and resistive to oxidation	Simeon	Hearing	
Carbuncle	A garnet, red, precious stone that also is an abrasive (used for smoothing and polishing)	Levi	To be joined to; to abide with	

Let's dissect the meaning of this first row of stones. Study Table II as the revelation of God unfolds. Take for instance, the first stone, *sardius*, which is a hard, tough stone that can be used for smoothing and polishing. Then, take a look at the meaning of the name Reuben, which was Israel's first born, *"behold a son."* And then take a look at the blessing bestowed upon Reuben at the time of his father's death, "... *my first born, my might, and the beginning of my strength, the excellency of dignity, and ... power."*

God is saying here: first of all, behold My son. Through Him there will come the smoothing and polishing your life requires. He's the excellency of dignity, meaning He occupies the position of the highest ranking order. Philippians 2:9–11 says, *"Wherefore God also hath highly exalted him, and given him a name which is above every name: that at the name of Jesus every knee should bow, of things in heaven, and things in earth, and things under the earth; and that every tongue should confess that Jesus Christ is Lord, to the glory of God the Father."*

Isn't this awesome! He is saying to us, behold My Son, who is highly exalted above everything that has been created. Through Him strength and power comes, because He's Lord.

Now, let's look at the second stone in the first row. It's a *topaz*, and its corresponding son's name is Simeon, which means *hearing*. In Matthew 17, when Christ was transfigured, the voice of God spoke out of a cloud and said, *"This is my beloved Son, in whom I am well pleased; hear ye him."* The Scriptures also say in Romans 10:17 that *faith cometh by hearing, and hearing by the word of God*. John 1:1–4 says: *"In the beginning was the Word, and the Word was with God, and the Word was God. The same was in the beginning with God. All things were made by him; and without him was not any thing made that was made. In Him was life; and the life was the light of men."* Logos is Greek for *word*; and the Greek definition of *logos* is *the intelligence, spoken*. Therefore John 1:1–4 is saying that in the beginning was the intelligence and Jesus Christ, the intelligence and the expressed image of that intelligence, was the life and light of men. That life and light came to show mankind the way back to God and to eternal life. Therefore, *"hear ye Him."*

Now let's look at what the properties of the topaz represent. A topaz is a salt of aluminum. Webster's dictionary states that aluminum is the most abundant element in the earth's crust. It is also a metallic element with good electrical and thermal conductivity, high reflectivity, and is resistant to oxidation. The dictionary stated that electrical conductivity (the ability to conduct electricity) is that entity in nature that consists of a positive and negative force that will either attract or repel when encountered by friction. Thermal conductivity is related to heat (energy that causes a substance's

Chapter Two

temperature to rise, fuse, evaporate or expand). The capacity to have high reflectivity is the ability to return a light or a sound wave from a surface. The ability to be resistant to oxidation is the ability to resist being changed to another element.

When I received the revelation of what God was saying regarding the benefits of hearing His Son, I almost jumped out of my chair. He revealed to me that hearing His Son will give me the ability to:

1) attract the positive and repel the negative when I encounter friction; and during the trials of life rise to every occasion as I become one with Christ Jesus and therefore one with God
2) in the midst of evil have the joy of being hidden in the secret place, and sit on a rock until the storm is over
3) have my boundaries increased as my way is re-established; and after going through my wilderness
4) have the ability to be a light to this dying world through which the image of Jesus Christ shines
5) have the ability to stand in faith during adversity without wavering

All of this through hearing God's Son!

This discovery brought to mind several other Scriptures: Philippians 4:13; Psalm 91:1; 1 Chronicles 4:10; John 17:13–21; James 4:7, 10.

The third stone in the first row is a *carbuncle*, which is a red, precious stone that is an abrasive used for smoothing and polishing. The corresponding son of Israel is Levi, his third born. Table II shows Levi means *to abide with, be joined to*. The Word of God in John 15 says, *"I am the true vine, and my Father is the husbandman . . . abide in me, and I in you, As the branch cannot bear fruit of itself, except it abide in the vine; no more can ye, except ye abide in me. . . . If ye abide in me, and my words abide in you, ye shall ask what ye will, and it shall be done unto you . . . If ye keep my commandments, ye shall abide in my love; even as I have kept my Father's commandments and abide in his love"*

Therefore the message of the first row of stones in the breastplate of judgment is: in order to become a jewel that would be flawless in the eyes of God we must:

1) first recognize that Jesus Christ, His son, is the excellency of dignity and power
2) listen to the voice of His Son and then
3) be joined to and abide with Him, because without Him we can do nothing

CHAPTER 3

TABLE III

STONES	STONE'S PROPERTIES	SON OF ISRAEL	MEANING OF NAME	BLESSING OF JACOB ON HIS SONS (GENESIS 49)
		Second Row		
Emerald	A beryl, which is a salt of beryllium and aluminum used as a hardening agent in alloy (a metal mixed with a more valuable metal to give it durability)	Judah	Praise	Thy hand shall be in the neck of thine enemies
Sapphire	A corundum; massive crystal used as an abrasive (smoothing and polishing agent)	Dan	To Judge	Shall judge his people
Diamond	One of the hardest stones in the world; used as an abrasive for smoothing and polishing	Naphtali	My Wrestling	Is a hind let loose; he giveth goodly words

Table III, the second row of stones, reveals additional attributes required to be God's ensign in the battle. Those requirements are praise, good judgment, and wrestling. Let's see what God reveals in this second row.

The first stone in the second row is an *emerald*, which bears the name of Judah, meaning *praise*. Note in Table III that Jacob predicted that the hand of Judah, or praise, shall be at the neck of his enemy. As we all know, the brain is the command post for all the functions of the body. The body can't function without it. In the neck there is a large blood vessel that carries blood to the brain. That blood contains the oxygen and nutrients needed for the brain to function. When there is something that hinders the blood from passing through that vessel, like the constriction of a hand, the brain will eventually die. Through our praise we will keep our hands at the neck of our adversary, rendering him powerless to function against us. Jesus said in John 10:10, "*The thief cometh not, but for to steal, and to kill and to destroy; I am come that they might have life, and that they might have it more abundantly.*" God encouraged our hearts in Hebrews 4:16–17 by saying, "*. . . we have not an high priest which cannot be touched with the feelings of our infirmities; but was in all points tempted like as we are, yet without sin. Let us therefore come boldly unto the throne of grace that we may obtain mercy, and find grace to help in time of need.*"

Therefore, we've been admonished by Psalm 100 to "*enter into His gates with thanksgiving, and into his courts with praise, be thankful unto him, and bless his name.*" Why? "*. . . for the Lord is good; his mercy is everlasting; and his truth endureth to all generations.*" Psalm 66:1–3 tells us to "*Make a joyful noise unto God, all ye lands; sing forth the honor of his name; make his praise glorious. Say unto God, how terrible art thou in thy works! Through the greatness of thy power shall thine enemies submit themselves unto thee.*"

You can only praise someone who you know is capable of coming to your aid; accomplishing that which is needed; and who is capable of assuring it does not change. Therefore, the pre-requisite for praising God is faith in God. Faith coupled with praise is a weapon against our adversary, the devil.

If you will note in the table an emerald is a salt of beryllium and aluminum. Beryllium is a strong metallic element used in alloys as a hardening agent, and, as I mentioned, aluminum has very valuable properties. Therefore, just as beryllium adds hardness and durability to aluminum, so does praise add strength and endurance to our faith. Remember it says in Hebrews 11:6, *without faith it is impossible to please Him . . .*

The second stone in this row is a *sapphire*, which is a massive abrasive. Remember, an abrasive can be utilized to smooth and to polish an object. When an abrasive is utilized to smooth and polish a surface, friction is employed. Friction also occurs when people disagree. Let's examine how an abrasive correlates with the name of its corresponding son of Israel.

The sapphire bears the name of Dan, which means to judge. Jacob said of his son, Dan, that he would judge his people. First Corinthians 6 says, *"know ye not that the saints shall judge the world? And if the world shall be judged by you, are ye unworthy to judge the smallest matters? Know ye not that we shall judge angels? How much more things that pertain to this life?"* The word *judge* means to be able to discern between good and evil and to pronounce a verdict or an opinion. The definition of that word contains a deeper meaning. *Discern* not only means to have the insight toward what God reveals as right and wrong; but to use that information wisely.

A wise man is not only marked by keen discernment, but by having knowledge and deep understanding. How will we obtain these treasures? In Proverbs 2 God tells us, *". . . if thou wilt receive my words, and hide my commandments with thee; so that thou incline thine ear unto wisdom, and apply thine heart to understanding . . . Then shalt thou understand the fear of the Lord, and find the knowledge of God."* This Scripture is telling us the only way we're going to be able to judge righteously regarding the issues of life, whether they are issues pertaining to our families or issues pertaining to terrorism and world peace, is that we must use the Word of God as our guide. Only the Word of God brings clarity and discernment.

What reward will we receive for seeking after wisdom, knowledge, and understanding? The third chapter of Proverbs tells us, *". . . length of days, and long life, and peace, shall they add to thee."* This chapter also admonishes us to let mercy and truth be an integral part of our being; because through them we will find favor and good understanding in the sight of God and man. In other words, *". . . in all thy ways acknowledge Him and He will direct thy path."*

Therefore, our ability to judge according to God's standards will be a massive, abrasive tool in this battle for salvation to reign.

Our third stone in row two is a *diamond*, and it bears the name of Naphtali, meaning *my wrestling*. Rachel said in Genesis 30:8 when she named Naphtali, *"with great wrestling have I wrestled with my sister and I have prevailed."*

Wrestling, for the Christian, is a mindset of devoting violent, serious effort or energy toward overthrowing our opponent, no matter what difficulties are presented. Matthew 11:12 says that the kingdom of heaven suffers violence and the violent take it by force. This verse is telling us that the place where God reigns, whether it's in the individual heart or in the royal priesthood as a whole, suffers violence. That violence comes from our age-old opponent, the devil. Violence requires violence. Therefore, we, the royal priesthood, must take and maintain the kingdom by force.

First Peter 5:8 says, *"be sober, be vigilant; because your adversary the devil, as a roaring lion, walketh about, seeking whom he may devour: whom resist steadfast in the faith, knowing that the same afflictions are accomplished in your brethren that are in the world."*

This Scripture tells us that the devil is crafty and cunning, and that he walks about seeking whom he may devour. Note the Scripture says <u>may</u> devour. That means he must have permission. And how do we know that he must get our permission? Because Luke 10:19 says that God has given us all power over the power of the enemy.

Therefore, if he is devouring any aspect of our lives, we have laid down our power and have given him permission. That same Scripture also admonishes us to be sober and vigilant. In other words, be temperate and balanced in all things; be calm; unhurried and watchful. These attributes will disarm the devil because he doesn't know what you're going to do. You're not giving him any clues to your tactics.

However, Ephesians 6:11 lays out the tactics God wants us to use during our wrestling.

Chapter Three

We are instructed to *"... put on the whole armor of God, that ye may be able to stand against the wiles of the devil. For we wrestle not against flesh and blood, but against principalities, against powers, against the rulers of the darkness of this world, against spiritual wickedness in high places. Wherefore take unto you the whole armor of God, that we may be able to withstand in the evil day, and having done all, to stand, stand therefore.,"*

We do this by:

1) having our loins (procreative power or your ability to bring forth) covered with truth
2) having on the breastplate of righteousness (shielding the heart, the seat of emotion, by conforming to all that God commands and appoints)
3) having our feet shod (bound) with the preparation of the gospel of peace. God admonishes us in 2 Timothy 2:15 to *"... study to show thyself approved unto God, a workman that needeth not to be ashamed, rightly dividing the word of truth."* Meaning? We are not to go anywhere and try to deliver the Word of God until we are prepared by studying His Word.
4) taking the shield of faith, wherewith we shall be able to quench all the fiery darts of the wicked

> *"Whosoever is born of God overcometh the world, and this is the victory that overcometh the world, even our faith"* (1 John 5:4).

This is a faith that believes God is who He says He is, and He can, and He will do what He says He will do.

5) take the helmet of salvation to protect the mind by believing God does deliver and save
6) take the sword of the spirit which is the Word of God

> "... for the word of God is quick and powerful, and sharper than any two-edged sword, piercing even the dividing asunder of soul and spirit, and of the joints and marrow, and is a discerner of the thoughts, and intents of the heart" (Hebrews 4:12).

7) praying always with all prayer and supplication in the Spirit

Once you have done this, you shall be like a hind let loose. You see, a hind is known for being swift and agile. Agility is marked by a ready ability to move with quick, easy grace. Therefore, the Word of God says in Habakkuk 3:19, "The Lord God is my strength and He will make my feet like hind's feet, and he will make me to walk upon my high places." The Word also says, "How beautiful upon the mountains are the feet of him that bringeth good tidings, that publisheth peace; that bringeth good tidings of good, that publisheth salvation; that saith unto Zion, Thy God reigneth!"

Our personal wrestling with life and Satan strengthens us, frees us up, and prepares us to be a soldier. I believe that's why Naphtali, meaning *my wrestling*, is represented by the hardest and most beautiful stone in the world, the diamond.

CHAPTER 4

TABLE IV

STONES	STONE'S PROPERTIES	SON OF ISRAEL	MEANING OF NAME	BLESSING OF JACOB ON HIS SONS (GENESIS 49)
		Third Row		
Ligure	Also called zircon; precious orange stone used in alloys, has the capacity to be resistant to corrosion	Gad	A Troop	He shall overcome at the last
Agate	Fine grained transparent crystal (A Quartz) used in industry to set right a frequency or keep it on course	Asher	Blessed	His bread shall be fat, and he shall yield royal dainties
Amethyst	Purple crystalized quartz, used as an abrasive as well as an agent used to set a frequency or keep it on course	Issachar	Hired for Payment	A Strong ass crouching down between two burdens.... And bowed his shoulder to bear and became a servant unto tribute

The third row of stones begins with a *liqure* or a *zircon*, which is an alloy that has the capacity to be resistant to corrosion. Remember, an alloy is a metal that is mixed with a more valuable metal so it can give that metal durability. Corrosion means to gradually wear away. Therefore, a zircon or liqure is an alloy that keeps something from wearing away. This stone represents Gad, the seventh son of Jacob. His name means *a troop* or *a group of soldiers* (men and women fit to contend with full strength, vigor, craft; with resources, in an extended contest or struggle). Also, his father Jacob predicted that *"He shall overcome at the last."*

Let's see what God is saying to us through this stone.

You know our God is awesome, because when King David was at Ziklag and the heads of the children of Israel came to assist him in battle, 1 Chronicles 12:8 said of the children of Gad: *"And of the*

Gadites there separated themselves unto David . . . men of war fit for the battle, that could handle shield and buckler, whose faces were like the faces of lions, and were as swift as the roes upon the mountains."

We have been called to be soldiers in the battle between good and evil. God needs dedicated soldiers in this battle for salvation to reign upon the land. First Timothy 6:12 says, *"Fight the good fight of faith, lay hold on eternal life, where unto thou are called . . ."* Jesus' commission for the saints, or his called-out soldiers, is found in John 17. In this chapter, Jesus said while praying in the Garden of Gethsemane, *". . . As thou has sent me into the world, even so have I also sent them into the world."* The Bible also states in Luke 24, *". . . that repentance and remission of sins should be preached in His name among all nations, beginning at Jerusalem."* Therefore, we have been given the directive in 2 Timothy 2:3 to *". . . endure hardness as a good soldier of Jesus Christ;"* and in 1 Timothy 1:8–9: *". . . be thou a partaker of the afflictions of the gospel according to the power of God; who hath saved us, and called us with a holy calling, not according to our works, but according to his own purpose and grace, which was given us in Christ Jesus before the world began . . ."*

And how do we endure hardness, be a partaker? In Psalm 18 David said that he kept the ways of the Lord and did not wickedly depart from God. He was also upright and kept himself from iniquity. Therefore God recompensed him according to his righteousness and the cleanness of his hands. What was the reward he received? David said, *"It is God that girdeth me with strength, and maketh my way perfect. He maketh my feet like hinds feet, and setteth me upon my high places. He teacheth my hands to war, so that a bow of steel is broken by mine arms. . . . I have pursued mine enemies, and overtaken them . . ."*

In 1 Corinthians 9:25–27 Paul teaches us how to be a soldier. That Scripture says, *". . . every man that striveth for the mastery is temperate in all things"* (that is, use moderation in everything that is done). Then he goes on to say, *"I therefore so run, not as*

Chapter Four

uncertainly; so fight I, not as one that beateth the air" (meaning we are not to fight as one who just flings his arms in mid air without purpose or direction. If we do, our efforts can be ambushed by the enemy). But Paul went on to say, *". . . But I keep under my body, and bring it into subjection."* In other words, Paul admonishes us to take control over the members of our body (every thought, every movement, and every desire), and not just have them flinging in the air where the enemy can ambush them; but utilize them totally for God's purpose.

He further instructs us by saying, *"No man that warreth entangleth himself with the affairs of this life; that he may please him who hath chosen him to be a soldier"* (2 Timothy 2:4). Here Paul is telling us that a soldier for God does not allow him or herself to become perplexed and bewildered in the midst of life's situations. There is no excuse for a state of confusion. We may be confused momentarily, but we have the Word of God to be our guide, because Psalm 119:105 says *"thy word is a lamp unto my feet and a light unto my path."*

Paul also instructs us to *". . . watch thou in all things, endure afflictions, do the work of an evangelist, make full proof of thy ministry."* And finally, in Hebrews 12:1–2 he tells us to, *". . . lay aside every weight, and the sin which doeth so easily beset us, and let us run with patience the race that is set before us, looking unto Jesus the author and finisher of our faith; who for the joy that was set before him endured the cross, despising the shame, and is set down at the right hand of the throne of God."* Thereby, overcoming!

God needs soldiers who will stand and fight. Soldiers who are not wimps, but who will use all their resources to endure and overcome. The breastplate of judgment has already revealed to us some of our resources (beholding Christ, hearing Christ, being joined to and abiding in Christ, praising God for who He is, utilizing righteous judgment, and utilizing the freedom and agility we gain from our spiritual wrestling). Therefore, we have been called to use those resources to be effective soldiers in God's army.

The second stone in the third row is an *agate*. An agate is a type of quartz. Remember, quartz is used to set right a frequency or keep that frequency on course. This stone represents the eighth son of Israel, who was born to him by Zilpah, Leah's maid. Leah said at the birth of this child, *"Happy am I, for the daughters will call me blessed."* So she named him Asher, meaning: *happy/blessed*. According to the Hebrew/Chaldee dictionary, written by James Strong, the word *asher* means to be straight, level, right and therefore, to prosper.

Some of the definitions of the word prosper include: to succeed, thrive, or flourish. In other words, to extensively develop, attain our goals, and then for everything to turn out well. I believe that the Lord correlated this stone with the name Asher because He wanted us to see in order for a soldier of Christ to stay on course and prosper in whatever he does; he must:

1. *Go in a straight path*: According to Deuteronomy 5:32–33 we are to observe and to do as the Lord has commanded us. We're not to turn aside to the right or to the left. We're to walk in all the ways that He has commanded so that we may live, prolong our days, and that it may be well with us. Several Scriptures come to mind that will help us do this: Proverbs 4:26–27, Joshua 1:8, Jeremiah 6:16. These Scriptures are telling us that our mouths should be filled with God's law and we should meditate on it day and night. Not only that, we should ponder the path of our feet. In other words, we as soldiers of Christ are not to do things haphazardly. Every move we make must be made with God's purpose in mind. And finally, if we become confused, Jeremiah 6:16 tells us to, *"Stand ye in the ways, and see, and ask for the old path, where is the good way, and walk therein . . ."* This Scripture is

instructing us to stand right where we are in the situation that life has dealt us; and see (face the situation and don't bury our heads). And then after we face the situation and see it for what it truly is, ask for the old way, which is God's way.

2. Be level (steady, unwavering, calm, reasonable, and balanced). We are not to vacillate between choices, but know what the will of God is. We're not to be easily moved or upset; but to be constant in God's purpose, utilizing direct and sure movements without turmoil or agitation. In every decision we make we're to use sound judgment, which comes from the leading of the Lord. And finally, we're to strive for balance in all aspects of our lives, not placing more inferences on one area than the other. In so doing stability is created. Remember, 1 Corinthians 15:58 says, *"Therefore my beloved brethren be steadfast immovable always abounding in the work of the Lord knowing that your labor is not in vain in the Lord."*

3. *Be right in his motives and actions*: The Word says that man looks at the outer appearance, but God looks at the heart. In other words, God knows our motives for doing what we do. He knows if we're truly serving Him; or if we're trying to get the glory or recognition for ourselves.

Matthew 5 and Deuteronomy 28 depict how we can obtain other spiritual and natural blessings.

The third stone in the third row is an *amethyst*. You will note, as we study the meaning of this stone, that it contains a lot of requirements to be one of God's precious jewels. First of all, let's look at the properties of an amethyst. The amethyst is a purple quartz. Purple is the color of royalty, and quartz is a stone that is utilized to keep a frequency on course. And if your mind is as curious as mine, you want to know what frequency God is talking about that has to be kept on course. Why did God demand that a purple quartz be used? We have already established that the color purple represents royalty; and in 1 Peter 2:9 God called us "*. . . a chosen generation, a royal priesthood.*" Next, we have to understand that a frequency is a periodic function that repeats the same sequence of values. And then we must remember that the Word of God says in Exodus 19:5–6, "*If you would obey my voice indeed, and keep my covenant, then ye shall be a peculiar treasure unto me above all people: for all the earth is mine; and ye shall be unto me a kingdom of priests, and a holy nation . . .*" The functions that God is calling us to continuously repeat are: obeying His voice and keeping His covenant. And what will be the reward for keeping that frequency on course? We will be His kingdom of priests, His holy nation.

Next, we need to focus on what are our responsibilities as a kingdom of priests. According to God's Word some of the responsibilities are:

1) show forth God's praise (Exodus 19:6)
2) offer up spiritual sacrifices acceptable to God (1 Peter 2:5) such as yielding ourselves unto God, and our members as instruments of righteousness (Romans 6:13); presenting our bodies as living sacrifices holy and acceptable unto God which is our reasonable service (Romans 12:1)
3) function in the ministry of reconciliation (1 Corinthians 5:18–19)
4) maintain dominion over Satan and one day, reign with Christ over the earth

Next, let's look at the name of the son of Israel that the amethyst represents. That name is Issachar, which means *hired for payment* or *to be compensated for services rendered* according to a contract.

Chapter Four

Now, let's focus on the meaning of that name and how it relates to us today. Christ's reward for His mission and life is a perfect example of being compensated for His services rendered unto God. Philippians 2 states, *". . . God hath highly exalted him, and given him a name which is above every name: that at the name of Jesus every knee should bow, of things in heaven, and things in earth, and things under the earth; and that every tongue should confess that Jesus Christ is Lord, to the glory of God the Father."* That same chapter admonishes us to follow in His footsteps by letting *"this mind be in you, which was also in Christ Jesus: who being in the form of God thought it not robbery to be equal with God: but made himself of no reputation, and took upon him the form of a servant, and was made in the likeness of men; and being found in fashion as a man, he humbled himself, and became obedient unto death, even the death of the cross.*" Jesus said in John 17:22–23 that the glory God the Father had given him, He has given to us so we may be made perfect in one; Jesus in us and God in him. Also, we are to remember what Romans 8:11 says," . . . *"if the Spirit of him that raised up Jesus from the dead dwell in you, he that raised up Christ shall also quicken your mortal bodies by his Spirit that dwelleth in you."* Therefore, even though the power exists within us, our mindset should be like Christ's mindset. Note that Israel said his son was as strong as an ass, which means he had strength and the power to bear. He not only had strength, he bowed his shoulder to bear and became a servant unto tribute. In other words, he humbled himself. Just as our savior made Himself of no reputation and became obedient until death, we are to do the same. This sounds like a tall order for a mere human being, but we have to remember it's not us who live the life, it is Christ living within us. Therefore, it's the humble heart and the obedient spirit that will keep us on course.

CHAPTER 5
TABLE V

STONES	STONE'S PROPERTIES	SON OF ISRAEL	MEANING OF NAME	BLESSING OF JACOB ON HIS SONS (GENESIS 49)
		Fourth Row		
Beryl	A salt of beryllium and aluminum used as a hardening agent in alloy (a metal mixed with a more valuable metal to give it durability)	Zebulun	To Dwell With	Shall dwell at the haven of the sea; and he shall be for a haven of ships; and his border shall be unto zidon
Onyx	Translucent quartz in parallel layers of different colors; used to set right a frequency or keep it on course	Joseph	The Lord Shall Add	Fruitful bough whose branches run over the wall
Jasper	Translucent quartz of many colors, especially green: used to set right a frequency or keep it on course	Benjamin	Son of the Right Hand	Shall ravin as a wolf in the morning shall devour the prey and at night he shall divide the spoil

Now we have come to the fourth and last row of stones in the breastplate of judgment. The Lord mandated that its first stone should be a *beryl*, which can be used as a hardening agent in an alloy. Remember, an alloy is a metal mixed with a more valuable metal to give it durability. Keep this thought in mind as God unfolds for us another requirement to be one of His precious jewels.

Zebulun was the tenth son born to Israel; his name means *to dwell with*. Israel predicted that Zebulun would dwell at the haven of the sea and shall be a haven for ships.

The word *haven* means a harbor (a place of security, comfort, refuge and shelter). It also means a *covering*. In Jeremiah 32:37 the Lord made a promise to the children of Israel. He said: *"Behold I will gather them out of all countries, whether I have driven them in mine anger; and in my fury, and in great wrath; and I will bring them again unto this place, and I will cause them to dwell safely."* This Scripture not only pertains to the descendants of Israel, but according to Isaiah 56:6–7, all those who join themselves to the Lord will dwell safely.

During these trying times when terrorists are on the loose, and there are wars and rumors of wars, when parents are killing children and children are killing parents, God promised in Proverbs 1:33 that; *"Whoso hearkeneth unto me shall dwell safely, and shall be quiet from fear of evil."* God also promised in Psalm 91 that, *"He that dwelleth in the secret place of the Most High shall abide under the shadow of the Almighty."* And where is this secret place? Psalm 27:5 reveals the answer: *"For in the time of trouble he shall hide me in his pavilion: in the secret of his tabernacle shall he hide me; he shall set me up upon a rock."*

Therefore, that secret place is in His tabernacle, or, in other words, in that place where you meet with Him; where you commune and sup with Him. And that is where He will set you upon a rock. And what is that rock? According to Ephesians 2:20–22, Christ is that rock, our chief cornerstone. The Word says that we the church *"are built upon the foundation of the apostles and prophets, Jesus Christ himself being the chief corner stone."* These Scriptures refer to the church as the building or temple of God and to the teachings of the apostles and prophets as the foundation of the church with Christ as its chief cornerstone. What significance does a foundation and a chief cornerstone have to a building? The foundation is the lowest structure of a building that supports the building and keeps it from sinking; and the cornerstone is the stone from which the building is aligned. Note in Matthew 16:16–18 where Christ asked Peter, *"Whom say ye that I am?"* Peter replied, *"Thou art the Christ, the son of the living God."* In those Scriptures Jesus said; *". . . upon this rock I will build my church; and the gates of hell will not prevail against it."* I believe this Scripture is referring to the rock as the knowledge and the acceptance that Jesus Christ is the Son of the living God. Against that rock, the gates of hell shall not prevail; thus creating a dwelling place of safety.

Just as Christ is our haven, we are to be His representatives in the land. It is our job as His representatives to be a haven for those who have been tossed on the seas of life. The Lord said He will gather those He has scattered, so they may dwell safely. Christ through us is compelling them to come into the ark of safety where they can be free from condemnation; where they can bring their wounded hearts for healing without fear of further injury.

The apostle Paul said in 1 Corinthians 9:22: *"To the weak became I as weak, that I might gain the weak: I am made all things to all men, that I might by all means save some."* James 5 states: *"Let him know, that he which converteth the sinner from the error of his way shall save a soul from death, and shall hide a multitude of sin."* The Bible also states in 1 Peter 4:8, *"And above all things have fervent charity [love] among yourselves; for charity shall cover a multitude of sins."*

We don't want to waste everything we have gained through our battles by destroying the spoil. We have learned to be instrumental in furthering God's plan for the redemption of man. We don't want to destroy them after they have come into the safe harbor. The beryl was chosen to be a part of the breastplate of judgment because it has the capacity to be a hardening agent in an alloy. Therefore, if we are to be a precious beryl in the eyes of God, we have to help our weaker brothers endure. God promised them that they will be able to dwell safely—we don't want to be the object of His wrath by wounding the apples of His eye. God's plan for the redemption of man will be fulfilled, whether we individually cooperate or not. It is our job to help them to endure.

The second stone in the last row is an *onyx*. The onyx is a translucent quartz, made in parallel layers, and comes in different colors. Remember, a quartz is a mineral that has the capacity to set right a frequency or keep it on course. Translucent means permitting the passage of light; or it can also mean, free from disguise or falseness. The word *parallel* means, extended in the same direction with all parts equally distant and equal in all essential parts. Parallel also means running in accordance with something. And to me the capacity to come in different colors represents diversity. A revelation is being disclosed just by stating the stone's properties. Let's see what else God will reveal regarding the onyx and its corresponding son of Israel.

This stone represents Joseph; his father said of him, *"Joseph is a fruitful bough, even a fruitful bough by a well; whose branches run over the wall . . ."* Israel also said of his son Joseph that he was sorely grieved, shot at, and hated. *"But his bow abode in strength, and the arms of his hands were made strong by the hands of the mighty God of Jacob (from thence is the shepherd, the stone of Israel.)"*

Webster's dictionary states that a bough is a branch of a tree. In John 15:5 Jesus said, *"I am the vine, ye are the branches: He that abideth in me, and I in him, the same bringeth forth much fruit: for without me ye can do nothing."* Jesus also said in John 15:1–3, *"I am the true vine, and my Father is the husbandman. Every branch in me that beareth not fruit he taketh away: and every branch that beareth fruit, he purgeth it, that it may bring forth more fruit. Now ye are clean [purged] through the word which I have spoken unto you. Abide in me, and I in you. As the branch cannot bear fruit of itself, except it abide in the vine; no more can ye, except ye abide in me."*

These Scriptures are stating that God is the husbandman or vinedresser, and Jesus Christ is the vine. Webster's dictionary states that a vine climbs by tendrils along the ground; and gives nourishment and life to its branches. And we, the church, are the branches that are to bring forth fruit.

Now, let's analyze John 15:1–3 a little further. The Scripture says that the gardener plucks off every branch that does not bring forth fruit. He purges or cleans the branch that brings forth fruit

Chapter Five

so that it will bring forth more fruit. And how does he clean the branch? That Scripture goes on to say we are cleansed through the words that He has spoken. And how can we be cleansed through the Word? Hebrews 4:12 says, *"For the word of God is quick, and powerful, and sharper than any two-edged sword, piercing even to the dividing asunder of soul and spirit, and of the joints and marrow, and is a discerner of the thoughts and intents of the heart."* The lexical aid to the New Testament, written by Spiros Zodiates, has comparative definitions of the words *spirit* and *soul*. It says that, "Spirit is the element in man which gives him the ability to think of God. It is man's vertical window, while soul is man's horizontal window making him conscious of his environment . . . soul is the element of life whereas spirit is the element of faith." There are issues in life—whether they are ethical, moral or spiritual—that befuddle our minds, make us stymied, and even blind us to the motives of our actions. But God said that His Word is sharper than any two-edged sword, meaning that it cuts both coming and going; revealing our inner man; making us translucent. Not only does the Word make things clearer, it also reveals our motives for doing things. And most of all, it reveals the truth.

Now let's examine the next property of the onyx. It's made in parallel layers. Remember, the word *parallel* means extended in the same direction, with all parts equally distant and equal in all essential parts. That definition brings to mind one of the properties of a vine: it climbs by tendrils. A tendril is a stem of the vine modified into a slender, spiraling, or coiling sensitive organ serving to attach the fruit to its support. We are to be that tendril that is attached to Christ, spiraling and weaving our way throughout the earth, bringing forth much fruit. In John 15:5 Jesus said, *"I am the vine, ye are the branches: He that abideth in me, and I in him, the same bringeth forth much fruit: for without me ye can do nothing."* The word *abide* means to dwell in, remain with, be steadfast with, or be attached to. John 15:10 also tells us how to abide in Christ:

"If ye keep my commandments, ye shall abide in my love; even as I have kept my Father's commandments, and abide in his love."

Now the gist of John 15 is that we the branches are to bring forth not only fruit, but much fruit. Jesus commanded His disciples in Mark 16 to, *"Go ye into all the world, and preach the gospel to every creature . . . And these signs shall follow them that believe; In my name shall they cast out devils; they shall speak with new tongues; they shall take up serpents; and if they drink any deadly thing, it shall not hurt them; they shall lay hands on the sick, and they shall recover . . ."* In verses 19 and 20, after Christ was received up into heaven and sat on the right hand of God, His disciples went forth and preached everywhere. The Lord was working with them, and confirmed the Word with signs, thereby bringing forth much fruit.

There are other fruits that we His branches must bring forth. The following Scriptures list several of those fruits. It is imperative that we study these fruits and emulate them, especially in these last days:

Galatians 5:16–26: (*love, joy, peace, longsuffering, gentleness, goodness, faith, meekness, temperance*)

2 Peter 1: 2–8: (*diligence, virtue, knowledge, patience, godliness, brotherly kindness, love*)

Matthew 3:1–12 (*fruits of repentance*)

Ephesians 5:9: (*righteousness and truth*)

The last stone in the breastplate of judgment is the *jasper*, a translucent quartz that comes in many colors. Remember, a quartz is a mineral that has the capacity to set right a frequency or keep it on course. Translucent means permitting the passage of light, or free from disguise or falseness. This stone represents Benjamin.

Chapter Five

Benjamin was the last son born to Israel; and was the only son he named. The name Benjamin means *son of the right hand.*

I was intrigued by the definition of Benjamin's name, because I know, according to Romans 8:34, Christ now sits at the right hand of the Father, continuously interceding for us. I did not know how the title, *son of the right hand*, related to me. Did God mean that I can be a son of His right hand or was the title just referring to Jesus? Then the Holy Spirit brought to mind Romans 8:17 which says, *"The Spirit itself beareth witness with our spirit, that we are the children of God: And if children, then heirs; heirs of God, and joint-heirs with Christ; if so be that we suffer with him, that we may be also glorified together."* This Scripture let me know as a child of God I am joint-heirs with Jesus Christ, sharing the same power and glory, and possessing the same inheritance—but only if I suffer with Him. Now, that's exciting. This Scripture inspired me to research further regarding my being the "son of the right hand."

During my research I noted in Matthew 25:31–40 Jesus prophesied that when the Son of Man comes He shall gather all nations and will separate the sheep from the goats; and will set the sheep on His right hand and the goats on the left. In my endeavor to understand the significance of being set on the right hand of Christ, I found that the Greek word for *right hand* is *dexios*. *Dexios* is the root word for several words: 1) *dexter*, meaning related to or situated on the right; 2) *dexterity*, meaning readiness and grace in physical activity and mental skill; and 3) *dexterous*, meaning mentally adroit and skillful. The word *adroit* means shrewdness, craft, or resourcefulness in coping with difficulty or danger. God began to illuminate my mind regarding the requirements to be this precious stone.

Further research revealed that the phrase *son of the right hand* not only implies skill, but exaltation and help. Note the following Scriptures: Acts 5:31 says, *"Him [Jesus] hath God exalted with his right hand to be a Prince and a Savior . . ."* Isaiah 41:10 reveals that help comes from the right hand of God: *"Fear thou not; for I am with thee: be not dismayed; for I am thy God: I will strengthen thee; yea, I will help thee; yea, I will uphold thee with the right hand of my righteousness."*

I also found that there is a reward for those who strive to be this precious stone. Israel said of his son Benjamin, *"he shall ravin [tear to pieces] as a wolf; and at night shall divide the spoil."* This prediction implies that he and his offspring will be conquerors and will reap the rewards of their battles. Remember, according to Galatians 3:27–29, we also are Abraham's seed. According to Revelation 22:12, Jesus will return quickly and bring with Him a reward for every man according to the work He has accomplished.

Now, let's see the requirements to be this precious jewel.

Matthew 25:34–36 went on to say, *"Then shall the King say unto them on his right hand, Come, ye blessed of my Father, inherit the kingdom prepared for you from the foundation of the world: For I was hungry, and ye gave me meat: I was thirsty, and ye gave me drink: I was a stranger, and ye took me in: Naked, and ye clothed me: I was sick, and ye visited me: I was in prison, and ye came unto me . . ."*

Isaiah 58:6–7 says: *"Is not this the fast that I have chosen? To loose the bands of wickedness, to undo the heavy burdens, and to let the oppressed go free, and that ye break every yoke?"*

In order to meet the requirements to be this precious jewel in God's eye, it's going to take skill. We're going to have to be keen with our perception and discernment. We're going to have to be skillful in planning and executing our plans to aid God in rescuing His creation. There is no doubt that God will enable us to do all these things, because the Word says that we can do all things through Christ. We're going to have to use our weapons of warfare. There is no time left for laziness, doubt, or procrastination. *"The harvest is truly plenteous"* and time is far spent.

Contact Information

REDEMPTION PRESS

To order additional copies of this book, please visit www.redemption-press.com.
Also available on Amazon.com and BarnesandNoble.com
Or by calling toll free 1-844-2REDEEM.

Lightning Source UK Ltd.
Milton Keynes UK
UKHW010825151022
410493UK00001B/1

9 781632 327390